# PRAYING AT EASTER

Donal Neary SJ

# Praying at Easter

the columba press

First published in 2011 by
the columba press
55A Spruce Avenue, Stillorgan Industrial Park,
Blackrock, Co Dublin

Cover designed by Bill Bolger
Origination by The Columba Press
Printed in Ireland by Brunswick Press Ltd, Dublin

ISBN 978-1-85607-731 6

# Contents

# Introduction

Easter is sometimes a forgotten season as soon as the Sunday is over; our book of reflections is to help us get involved and engaged in the mystery of the Lord's life which is called resurrection. This is the mystery of how he is alive among us today.

The scripture is taken from the gospel of the day, sometimes shortened. The reflection makes some link of prayer and life with the mystery of the risen Lord.

This link is relevant – because the resurrection is for now. Jesus' focus in his ministry was more on this life than the next; he spoke much more about this world than the next. Wherever we are lifted beyond selfish and self-centred cares, we are sharing the life of the risen Lord. We are 'ministers of the resurrection' where we bring about the kingdom of God – the kingdom of justice, peace, love, compassion and all the qualities Jesus embodied.

How to use the book:

- Read the scripture – silently or aloud.
- Notice what phrase may stay with you; let that echo in your mind and heart. Wonder about its meaning, and know that it was written by disciples or spoken by Jesus,

from this side of Easter – the only Christ they knew in the early church was the Risen Lord, and this is the Lord we know.

- The prayer is the same for each week; pray it or adapt it; and the reflection is one persons' thoughts on the scripture.

  This can be used as a reflection in liturgy, school assemblies, paraliturgies as well as in personal prayer.

Daily prayer over the Easter mystery opens us to the joy of the risen Lord, always offered to us, and to the challenge of being followers in a real sense of the risen Lord.

*Donal Neary SJ*

*Many of the reflections have been used, with some adaptation and revision, on the website Sacred Space www.sacredspace.ie and published in* Sacred Space: the prayer book *(2010 and 2011 editions), Michelle Anderson Publishing Pty Ltd, Melbourne, Australia, and used here with thanks and appreciation.*

# Easter Sunday

*John 20:1-9*

Early on the first day of the week, while it was still dark, Mary Magdalene came to the tomb and saw that the stone had been removed from the tomb. So she ran and went to Simon Peter and the other disciple, the one whom Jesus loved, and said to them, 'They have taken the Lord out of the tomb, and we do not know where they have laid him.' Then Peter and the other disciple set out and went toward the tomb. The two were running together, but the other disciple outran Peter and reached the tomb first. He bent down to look in and saw the linen wrappings lying there, but he did not go in. Then Simon Peter came, following him, and went into the tomb. He saw the linen wrappings lying there, and the cloth that had been on Jesus' head, not lying with the linen wrappings but rolled up in a place by itself. Then the other disciple, who reached the tomb first, also went in, and he saw and believed; for as yet they did not understand the scripture, that he must rise from the dead.

*Prayer*

Risen Lord, be compassionate in me with your
new life;
Be consoling and encouraging in me with your
risen love;
Be hopeful, loving and trusting in me and for
others
For you are Lord, raised in death, now and forever. Amen.

*Reflection*

The tomb was empty and for the faithful ones,
this was a sign of new life. Some would
remember Jesus saying he would rise from
death. Others would feel down, cheated or just
lost. Same with ourselves. The tough times of
life can bring us close to God, or distance us.
Suffering can make us better people, or make
us bitter and isolated. We may feel a bit of both
at times. The empty tomb is the message that
nothing is final in this life, not even death.
God's love is stronger than any human power,
violence or cruelty. Love conquers all.

## Week 1: Monday

*Matthew 28:8-15*

So the women left the tomb quickly with fear and great joy, and ran to tell his disciples. Suddenly Jesus met them and said, 'Greetings!' And they came to him, took hold of his feet, and worshipped him. Then Jesus said to them, 'Do not be afraid; go and tell my brothers to go to Galilee; there they will see me.'

*Prayer*

Risen Lord, be compassionate in me with your new life;

Be consoling and encouraging in me with your risen love;

Be hopeful, loving and trusting in me and for others

For you are Lord, raised in death, now and forever. Amen.

*Reflection*

We find God in the old and familiar places of life, as the apostles found him once again in Galilee. We find him in the memories of past love and the joys of present love. We find him in our tears and laughter, and in the lovely light of a morning sunrise. We can find him so often now, because the risen Lord is not bound by time or place. Alleluia!

## Week 1: Tuesday

*John 20:11-18*
But Mary stood weeping outside the tomb. As she wept, she bent over to look into the tomb; and she saw two angels in white, sitting where the body of Jesus had been lying, one at the head and the other at the feet. They said to her, 'Woman, why are you weeping?' She said to them, 'They have taken away my Lord, and I do not know where they have laid him.' When she had said this, she turned around and saw Jesus standing there, but she did not know that it was Jesus. Jesus said to her, 'Woman, why are you weeping? Whom are you looking for?' Supposing him to be the gardener, she said to him, 'Sir, if you have carried him away, tell me where you have laid him, and I will take him away.' Jesus said to her, 'Mary!' She turned and said to him in Hebrew, 'Rabbouni!' (which means Teacher). Jesus said to her, 'Do not hold on to me, because I have not yet ascended to the Father. But go to my brothers and say to them, "I am ascending to my Father and your Father, to my God and your God".' Mary Magdalene went and announced to the disciples, 'I have seen the Lord'; and she told them that he had said these things to her.

## *Prayer*

Risen Lord, be compassionate in me with your
new life;

Be consoling and encouraging in me with your
risen love;

Be hopeful, loving and trusting in me and for
others

For you are Lord, raised in death, now and forever. Amen.

## *Reflection*

Have you seen the Lord? Somehow like Mary,
we may glimpse the Lord. Seeing may not be
physical but we see him in the light of love, the
colour of care, the beauty of compassion, the
energy of service. In all that is human we see
and sense the Lord. Mary's mood changed
from tears to joy; all she needed was the presence of the Lord, now and always, raised from
death.

## Week 1: Wednesday

*Luke 24:13-35*

They said to each other, 'Were not our hearts burning within us while he was talking to us on the road, while he was opening the scriptures to us?' That same hour they got up and returned to Jerusalem; and they found the eleven and their companions gathered together. They were saying, 'The Lord has risen indeed, and he has appeared to Simon!' Then they told what had happened on the road, and how he had been made known to them in the breaking of the bread.

*Prayer*

Risen Lord, be compassionate in me with your new life;

Be consoling and encouraging in me with your risen love;

Be hopeful, loving and trusting in me and for others

For you are Lord, raised in death, now and forever. Amen.

*Reflection*

Our footsteps all along the paths of our lives are matched by the footsteps of Jesus. Hearts burned and tears were dried as the risen Lord made his way into the lives of his followers. Prayer gives time for his word to enter deeply into our hearts, burning away selfishness and fear, leaving only the flame of love, tenderness and compassion.

## Week 1: Thursday

*Luke 24:35-48*

Then they told what had happened on the road, and how he had been made known to them in the breaking of the bread. While they were talking about this, Jesus himself stood among them and said to them, 'Peace be with you.' They were startled and terrified, and thought that they were seeing a ghost. He said to them, 'Why are you frightened, and why do doubts arise in your hearts? Look at my hands and my feet; see that it is I myself. Touch me and see; for a ghost does not have flesh and bones as you see that I have.' And when he had said this, he showed them his hands and his feet.

*Prayer*

Risen Lord, be compassionate in me with your
new life;

Be consoling and encouraging in me with your
risen love;

Be hopeful, loving and trusting in me and for
others

For you are Lord, raised in death, now and forever. Amen.

*Reflection*

The common greeting of Jesus to his followers
is the wish for peace. In prayer that is his word
to us. He knocks at our door, with this word:
'Peace be with you.' Prayer can bring peace in
turmoil and troubled times. He offers his peace
and asks his followers to be people who work
and pray for peace. Let peace be the word for
our prayer today – peace received and peace
prayed for.

## Week 1: Friday

*John 21:1-14*

When they had gone ashore, they saw a charcoal fire there, with fish on it, and bread. Jesus said to them, 'Bring some of the fish that you have just caught.' So Simon Peter went aboard and hauled the net ashore, full of large fish, a hundred and fifty-three of them; and though there were so many, the net was not torn. Jesus said to them, 'Come and have breakfast.' Now none of the disciples dared to ask him, 'Who are you?' because they knew it was the Lord. Jesus came and took the bread and gave it to them, and did the same with the fish. This was now the third time that Jesus appeared to the disciples after he was raised from the dead.

*Prayer*

Risen Lord, be compassionate in me with your new life;

Be consoling and encouraging in me with your risen love;

Be hopeful, loving and trusting in me and for others

For you are Lord, raised in death, now and forever. Amen.

*Reflection*

Imagine yourself walking on a beach towards a group around a fire. The smell of breakfast is in the air. You realise that it is Jesus and his group of followers. He has been raised from death. As you come near the group, you notice that Jesus turns towards you and you hear his invitation, 'Come and have breakfast' – a gentle call of God.

## Week 1: Saturday

*Mark 16:9-15*

Now after he rose early on the first day of the week, he appeared first to Mary Magdalene, from whom he had cast out seven demons. She went out and told those who had been with him, while they were mourning and weeping. But when they heard that he was alive and had been seen by her, they would not believe it. After this he appeared in another form to two of them, as they were walking into the country. And they went back and told the rest, but they did not believe them. Later he appeared to the eleven themselves as they were sitting at the table; and he upbraided them for their lack of faith and stubbornness, because they had not believed those who saw him after he had risen. And he said to them, 'Go into all the world and proclaim the good news to the whole creation.'

### Prayer

Risen Lord, be compassionate in me with your new life;

Be consoling and encouraging in me with your risen love;

Be hopeful, loving and trusting in me and for others

For you are Lord, raised in death, now and forever. Amen.

### Reflection

Faith in the risen Christ came slowly to some if not all of the apostles. It took more than a few occasions and apparitions to convince them that the Lord had risen from death. All faith has its ups and downs; prayer has its good times and tough times. Faith grows in a trust in God that he is always near, though he may not seem so. It is sometimes a dark love; and the love in the darkness is what brings faith to life.

## Second Sunday of Easter

*John 20:19-31*

When it was evening on that day, the first day of the week, and the doors of the house where the disciples had met were locked for fear of the Jews, Jesus came and stood among them and said, 'Peace be with you.' After he said this, he showed them his hands and his side. Then the disciples rejoiced when they saw the Lord. Jesus said to them again, 'Peace be with you. As the Father has sent me, so I send you.' When he had said this, he breathed on them and said to them, 'Receive the Holy Spirit. If you forgive the sins of any, they are forgiven them; if you retain the sins of any, they are retained.' But Thomas (who was called the Twin), one of the twelve, was not with them when Jesus came. So the other disciples told him, 'We have seen the Lord.' But he said to them, 'Unless I see the mark of the nails in his hands, and put my finger in the mark of the nails and my hand in his side, I will not believe.' A week later his disciples were again in the house, and Thomas was with them. Although the doors were shut, Jesus came and stood among them and said, 'Peace be with you.' Then he said to Thomas, 'Put your finger here and see my hands. Reach out your hand and put it in my side. Do not doubt but believe.' Thomas answered him, 'My Lord and my God!' Jesus said to him, 'Have you believed because you have seen me? Blessed are those who have not seen and yet have come to believe.'

### Prayer

Lord, strengthen my faith;
In times of weakness give me confidence in your gift of faith to me,
In times of confusion, give me your gift of meaning in life,
In good times and bad, give me I ask, the joy of faith. Amen.

### Reflection

In community, the disciples found faith in the risen Christ. Thomas for some reason was not with them when the Lord came. Separated from the community, he found faith more difficult. Faith in the Lord, while personal, is not a private affair. Through the faith of one, the faith of another may be strengthened. Formation in faith for the disciples had its communal dimension – together they learned and found faith in the Lord.

## Week 2: Monday

*John 3:1-8*

Now there was a Pharisee named Nicodemus, a leader of the Jews. He came to Jesus by night and said to him, 'Rabbi, we know that you are a teacher who has come from God; for no one can do these signs that you do apart from the presence of God.' Jesus answered him, 'Very truly, I tell you, no one can see the kingdom of God without being born from above.' Nicodemus said to him, 'How can anyone be born after having grown old? Can one enter a second time into the mother's womb and be born?' Jesus answered, 'Very truly, I tell you, no one can enter the kingdom of God without being born of water and Spirit. What is born of the flesh is flesh, and what is born of the Spirit is spirit. Do not be astonished that I said to you, 'You must be born from above.' The wind blows where it chooses, and you hear the sound of it, but you do not know where it comes from or where it goes. So it is with everyone who is born of the Spirit.'

### *Prayer*

Lord, strengthen my faith;
In times of weakness give me confidence in your gift of faith to me,
In times of confusion, give me your gift of meaning in life,
In good times and bad, give me I ask, the joy of faith. Amen.

### *Reflection*

Prayer moments and times of faith are moments 'to be born from above'. We allow cares, no matter how important to ourselves and others, to drift off for a while. We switch off the phone and the texts, and allow God become real in our lives, for he already lives in our hearts. We are born strong with God, and with God's grace being born in us, love is born too. Prayer is our daily time to rekindle love in our lives.

## Week 2: Tuesday

*John 3:7-15*

Jesus said, 'Do not be astonished that I said to you, 'You must be born from above.' The wind blows where it chooses, and you hear the sound of it, but you do not know where it comes from or where it goes. So it is with everyone who is born of the Spirit.' Nicodemus said to him, 'How can these things be?' Jesus answered him, 'Are you a teacher of Israel, and yet you do not understand these things? Very truly, I tell you, we speak of what we know and testify to what we have seen; yet you do not receive our testimony. If I have told you about earthly things and you do not believe, how can you believe if I tell you about heavenly things? No one has ascended into heaven except the one who descended from heaven, the Son of Man. And just as Moses lifted up the serpent in the wilderness, so must the Son of Man be lifted up, that whoever believes in him may have eternal life.'

*Prayer*

Lord, strengthen my faith;
In times of weakness give me confidence in
your gift of faith to me,
In times of confusion, give me your gift of
meaning in life,
In good times and bad, give me I ask, the joy of
faith. Amen.

*Reflection*

When we look on the cross, it's a look of faith.
The man on it is a king and the cross is a
throne. It is no longer a thing of shame.
Looking on it we look on love; truly, a love
which suffered but its saving power is not in
the suffering that led Jesus there but in his love.
We are lifted up by love to look on the crucifix
and see in its starkness the eternal love of God.

## Week 2: Wednesday

*John 3:16-21*

For God so loved the world that he gave his only Son, so that everyone who believes in him may not perish but may have eternal life. Indeed, God did not send the Son into the world to condemn the world, but in order that the world might be saved through him. Those who believe in him are not condemned; but those who do not believe are condemned already, because they have not believed in the name of the only Son of God. And this is the judgement, that the light has come into the world, and people loved darkness rather than light because their deeds were evil. For all who do evil hate the light and do not come to the light, so that their deeds may not be exposed. But those who do what is true come to the light, so that it may be clearly seen that their deeds have been done in God.

*Prayer*

Lord, strengthen my faith;

In times of weakness give me confidence in your gift of faith to me,

In times of confusion, give me your gift of meaning in life,

In good times and bad, give me I ask, the joy of faith. Amen.

*Reflection*

Prayer may be compared to a time of opening ourselves in the light of God, like sunning ourselves in the warmth of the sun, the gentle and bright light which illuminates us completely. In prayer the light of God enters totally into a person in a way which lightens the burdens of life, and which shares light with others. It can help in prayer to imagine the light surrounding you and to be reminded that this light surrounds us outside prayer also. We walk, sit, lie down, wake and sleep in the atmosphere of the light of God.

## Week 2: Thursday

*John 3:31-36*

The one who comes from above is above all; the one who is of the earth belongs to the earth and speaks about earthly things. The one who comes from heaven is above all. He testifies to what he has seen and heard, yet no one accepts his testimony. Whoever has accepted his testimony has certified this, that God is true. He whom God has sent speaks the words of God, for he gives the Spirit without measure. The Father loves the Son and has placed all things in his hands. Whoever believes in the Son has eternal life; whoever disobeys the Son will not see life, but must endure God's wrath.

### Prayer

Lord, strengthen my faith;
In times of weakness give me confidence in your gift of faith to me,
In times of confusion, give me your gift of meaning in life,
In good times and bad, give me I ask, the joy of faith. Amen.

### Reflection

God's generosity is hinted at here – in all that he has given to Jesus, it is given without measure. God's hand always pours his gifts on us, especially the gift of the Holy Spirit, with the individual gifts of the Spirit. Ask in prayer for the gift you want; ask in the knowledge that every prayer is answered with a new love of God.

## Week 2: Friday

*John 6:1-15*

After hearing Jesus (promise his flesh to eat), many of his followers said: 'This is intolerable language. How could anyone accept it?' After this, many of his disciples went away and followed him no more. Then Jesus said to the Twelve: 'What about you, do you want to go away too?' Simon Peter answered: 'Lord, to whom shall we go? You have the message of eternal life, and we believe, we have come to know that you are the Holy One of God.'

*Prayer*

Lord, strengthen my faith;
In times of weakness give me confidence in your gift of faith to me,
In times of confusion, give me your gift of meaning in life,
In good times and bad, give me I ask, the joy of faith. Amen.

*Reflection*

The message of Jesus reaches into the depths of our humanity, into those spaces of life where we dance and sing, laugh and cry, mourn and despair, hope and love, and where everything deeply human dwells within us. Into that space Jesus also pours the living water and speaks an eternal word, and in prayer we can say 'You have the message of eternal life.'

## Week 2: Saturday

*John 6:16-21*

When evening came, his disciples went down to the sea, got into a boat, and started across the sea to Capernaum. It was now dark, and Jesus had not yet come to them. The sea became rough because a strong wind was blowing. When they had rowed about three or four miles, they saw Jesus walking on the sea and coming near the boat, and they were terrified. But he said to them, 'It is I; do not be afraid.' Then they wanted to take him into the boat, and immediately the boat reached the land toward which they were going.

*Prayer*

Lord, strengthen my faith;

In times of weakness give me confidence in your gift of faith to me,

In times of confusion, give me your gift of meaning in life,

In good times and bad, give me I ask, the joy of faith. Amen.

*Reflection*

His followers didn't realise that he was aware of them and caring for them even when it was dark all around and the wind was against them. Even before he came to them, walking on the storm, he had been watching for them and looking out for them. The same now – God is always on our side, always keeping an eye on us, even when he seems far away. Prayer opens the door to this trust and confidence.

## Third Sunday of Easter Year A

*Luke 24:13-35*

Then beginning with Moses and all the prophets, he interpreted to them the things about himself in all the scriptures. As they came near the village to which they were going, he walked ahead as if he were going on. But they urged him strongly, saying, 'Stay with us, because it is almost evening and the day is now nearly over.' So he went in to stay with them. When he was at the table with them, he took bread, blessed and broke it, and gave it to them. Then their eyes were opened, and they recognised him; and he vanished from their sight. They said to each other, 'Were not our hearts burning within us while he was talking to us on the road, while he was opening the scriptures to us?' That same hour they got up and returned to Jerusalem; and they found the eleven and their companions gathered together. They were saying, 'The Lord has risen indeed, and he has appeared to Simon!' Then they told what had happened on the road, and how he had been made known to them in the breaking of the bread.

## Prayer

Stay with me Lord in all I do and say,
Stay with me in the morning and evening of life,
Stay with me in the communion of love
And in the communion of the Eucharist. Amen.

## Reflection

Every table of the Eucharist is Emmaus; every moment of hearing the scriptures is the road to Emmaus. We are always on that road, as Jesus speaks his word and breaks the bread of his love. The words give meaning to life as his opening of the scriptures did for the disciples; the bread of life feeds us as he did on the table of their house. The words and the bread sent them into the community and to the world with their story of how they recognised him. Maybe the daily word and the daily bread can do the same for us.

## Third Sunday of Easter Year B

*Luke 24:35-48*

Then they told what had happened on the road, and how he had been made known to them in the breaking of the bread.

While they were talking about this, Jesus himself stood among them and said to them, 'Peace be with you.' They were startled and terrified, and thought that they were seeing a ghost. He said to them, 'Why are you frightened, and why do doubts arise in your hearts? Look at my hands and my feet; see that it is I myself. Touch me and see; for a ghost does not have flesh and bones as you see that I have.' And when he had said this, he showed them his hands and his feet. While in their joy they were disbelieving and still wondering, he said to them, 'Have you anything here to eat?' They gave him a piece of broiled fish, and he took it and ate in their presence.

Then he said to them, 'These are my words that I spoke to you while I was still with you – that everything written about me in the law of Moses, the prophets, and the psalms must be fulfilled.' Then he opened their minds to understand the scriptures, and he said to them, 'Thus it is written, that the Messiah is to suffer and to rise from the dead on the third day, and that repentance and forgiveness of sins is to be proclaimed in his name to all nations, beginning from Jerusalem. You are witnesses of these things.'

## Prayer

Stay with me Lord in all I do and say,
Stay with me in the morning and evening of life,
Stay with me in the communion of love
And in the communion of the Eucharist. Amen.

## Reflection

The common greeting of Jesus to his followers is the wish for peace. In prayer that is his word to us. He knocks at our door, with this word 'Peace be with you.' Prayer can bring peace in turmoil and troubled times. He offers his peace and asks his followers to be people who make peace. Let peace be the word for our prayer today – peace received and peace prayed for.

## Third Sunday of Easter Year C

*John 21 1-19*

After these things Jesus showed himself again to the disciples by the Sea of Tiberias; and he showed himself in this way. Gathered there together were Simon Peter, Thomas called the Twin, Nathanael of Cana in Galilee, the sons of Zebedee, and two others of his disciples. Simon Peter said to them, 'I am going fishing.' They said to him, 'We will go with you.' They went out and got into the boat, but that night they caught nothing.

Just after daybreak, Jesus stood on the beach; but the disciples did not know that it was Jesus. Jesus said to them, 'Children, you have no fish, have you?' They answered him, 'No.' He said to them, 'Cast the net to the right side of the boat, and you will find some.' So they cast it, and now they were not able to haul it in because there were so many fish. That disciple whom Jesus loved said to Peter, 'It is the Lord!' When Simon Peter heard that it was the Lord, he put on some clothes, for he was naked, and jumped into the lake. But the other disciples came in the boat, dragging the net full of fish, for they were not far from the land, only about a hundred yards off.

When they had gone ashore, they saw a charcoal fire there, with fish on it, and bread. Jesus said to them, 'Bring some of the fish that you have just caught.' So Simon Peter went aboard and hauled the net ashore, full of large fish, a hundred and fifty-three of them; and though there were so many, the net was not torn. Jesus said to them, 'Come and have breakfast.' Now none of the disciples dared to ask him, 'Who are you?' because they knew it was the Lord. Jesus came and took the bread and gave it to them, and did the same with the fish. This was now the third time that Jesus appeared to the disciples after he was raised from the dead.

## Prayer

Stay with me Lord in all I do and say,
Stay with me in the morning and evening of life,
Stay with me in the communion of love
And in the communion of the Eucharist. Amen.

## Reflection

Imagine yourself walking on a beach towards a group around a fire. The smell of breakfast is in the air. You realise that it is Jesus and his group of followers. He has been raised from death. As you come near the group, you notice Jesus turns towards you and you hear his invitation, 'Come and have breakfast'. Let that picture guide your prayer and faith today.

## Week 3: Monday

*John 6:22-29*

The next day the crowd that had stayed on the other side of the lake saw that there had been only one boat there. They also saw that Jesus had not got into the boat with his disciples, but that his disciples had gone away alone. Then some boats from Tiberias came near the place where they had eaten the bread after the Lord had given thanks. So when the crowd saw that neither Jesus nor his disciples were there, they themselves got into the boats and went to Capernaum looking for Jesus. When they found him on the other side of the lake, they said to him, 'Rabbi, when did you come here?' Jesus answered them, 'Very truly, I tell you, you are looking for me, not because you saw signs, but because you ate your fill of the loaves. Do not work for the food that perishes, but for the food that endures for eternal life, which the Son of Man will give you. For it is on him that God the Father has set his seal.' Then they said to him, 'What must we do to perform the works of God?' Jesus answered them, 'This is the work of God, that you believe in him whom he has sent.'

*Prayer*

Stay with me Lord in all I do and say,
Stay with me in the morning and evening of life,
Stay with me in the communion of love
And in the communion of the Eucharist. Amen.

*Reflection*

The big sign of God is in the life, works and words of Jesus Christ. The people wanted more bread, more miracles. The bread of Capernaum is not just flour and water – it is the word and love of God in Jesus. This work is in each of us too – his work is our faith. Let our prayer be a desire to believe more deeply – 'Lord I believe, strengthen my belief.'

## Week 3: Tuesday

*John 6:30-35*

So they said to him, 'What sign are you going to give us then, so that we may see it and believe you? What work are you performing? Our ancestors ate the manna in the wilderness; as it is written, "He gave them bread from heaven to eat".' Then Jesus said to them, 'Very truly, I tell you, it was not Moses who gave you the bread from heaven, but it is my Father who gives you the true bread from heaven. For the bread of God is that which comes down from heaven and gives life to the world.' They said to him, 'Sir, give us this bread always.' Jesus said to them, 'I am the bread of life. Whoever comes to me will never be hungry, and whoever believes in me will never be thirsty.'

*Prayer*

Stay with me Lord in all I do and say,
Stay with me in the morning and evening of life,
Stay with me in the communion of love
And in the communion of the Eucharist. Amen.

*Reflection*

All we need for happiness and fulfilment is in
the teaching and the love of God. The bread
from heaven is the word of God and the
Eucharist. With the food of this teaching, nothing else is needed for living in the truth. Prayer
can be a time of being grateful to God for this
word of life, and for this bread which means
that God is never far away from us. The word
and the bread nourish us all the days of life.

## Week 3: Wednesday

*John 6:35-40*

Jesus said to the people: 'I am the bread of life. Whoever comes to me will never be hungry, and whoever believes in me will never be thirsty.' But I have said to you that you have seen me and yet do not believe. Everything that the Father gives me will come to me, and anyone who comes to me I will never drive away; for I have come down from heaven, not to do my own will, but the will of him who sent me. And this is the will of him who sent me, that I should lose nothing of all he has given me, but raise it up on the last day. This is indeed the will of my Father, that all who see the Son and believe in him may have eternal life; and I will raise them up on the last day.'

## *Prayer*

Stay with me Lord in all I do and say,
Stay with me in the morning and evening of life,
Stay with me in the communion of love
And in the communion of the Eucharist. Amen.

## *Reflection*

The bread of life exists within the community of Jesus Christ. We, his people, are his bread. We are to be this bread for each other. The mystery of the Eucharist is of God being close to his people, and of his people being the body of Christ. We are baptised into Christ. Think in prayer this day of those close to us who need the nourishment and the comfort of the love of God and his care. Can we give it to them?

## Week 3: Thursday

*John 6:44-51*

No one can come to me unless drawn by the Father who sent me; and I will raise that person up on the last day. It is written in the prophets, 'And they shall all be taught by God.' Everyone who has heard and learned from the Father comes to me. Not that anyone has seen the Father except the one who is from God; he has seen the Father. Very truly, I tell you, whoever believes has eternal life. I am the bread of life. Your ancestors ate the manna in the wilderness, and they died. This is the bread that comes down from heaven, so that one may eat of it and not die. I am the living bread that came down from heaven. Whoever eats of this bread will live forever; and the bread that I will give for the life of the world is my flesh.'

### Prayer

Stay with me Lord in all I do and say,
Stay with me in the morning and evening of life,
Stay with me in the communion of love
And in the communion of the Eucharist. Amen.

### Reflection

We sort of live two lives – the flesh and the spirit, earthly and eternal. Faith in God is life-giving. It gives energy and nourishment to the everyday, to the commonplace and to the struggle to do good and live a gospel-centred life. Prayer is a time to be aware of the life which is eternal. Moments of prayer bring us in touch with the eternal within us, and the eternal around us, the atmosphere of the risen Christ.

## Week 3: Friday

*John 6:52-59*

The Jews then disputed among themselves, saying, 'How can this man give us his flesh to eat?' So Jesus said to them, 'Very truly, I tell you, unless you eat the flesh of the Son of Man and drink his blood, you have no life in you. Those who eat my flesh and drink my blood have eternal life, and I will raise them up on the last day; for my flesh is true food and my blood is true drink. Those who eat my flesh and drink my blood abide in me, and I in them. Just as the living Father sent me, and I live because of the Father, so whoever eats me will live because of me.'

### Prayer

Stay with me Lord in all I do and say,
Stay with me in the morning and evening of life,
Stay with me in the communion of love
And in the communion of the Eucharist. Amen.

### Reflection

Jesus is presented through this chapter of John's gospel as the giver of divine life. He possesses the fullness of Godly life. This is what he leaves to us in his flesh and blood, the Eucharist. Prayer unites us to the sacrifice of Jesus who through all his life, not just at Calvary, gave himself to us as teacher, healer, protector and always as loving friend. What is a favourite title of yours for Jesus – repeat that sometimes in prayer and bring it through the day like a favourite line of a song or a refrain of music.

## Week 3: Saturday 12

*John 6:60-69*

Because of his teaching, many of his disciples turned back and no longer went about with him. So Jesus asked the twelve, 'Do you also wish to go away?' Simon Peter answered him, 'Lord, to whom can we go? You have the words of eternal life. We have come to believe and know that you are the Holy One of God.'

## Prayer

Stay with me Lord in all I do and say,
Stay with me in the morning and evening of life,
Stay with me in the communion of love
And in the communion of the Eucharist. Amen.

## Reflection

The gift of Jesus is the life that underpins our
human life. He has become one of us so that we
become like him. His words lead us into a quality of life which gives meaning, hope and love
in all we do. Nobody else can give what he
gives – a full meaning of life, seen in the example of his life. Time with him is always time
well spent.

## Fourth Sunday of Easter Year A

*John 10:1-10*

Jesus said to the people: 'Very truly, I tell you, anyone who does not enter the sheepfold by the gate but climbs in by another way is a thief and a bandit. The one who enters by the gate is the shepherd of the sheep. The gatekeeper opens the gate for him, and the sheep hear his voice. He calls his own sheep by name and leads them out. When he has brought out all his own, he goes ahead of them, and the sheep follow him because they know his voice. They will not follow a stranger, but they will run from him because they do not know the voice of strangers.' Jesus used this figure of speech with them, but they did not understand what he was saying to them. So again Jesus said to them, 'Very truly, I tell you, I am the gate for the sheep. All who came before me are thieves and bandits; but the sheep did not listen to them. I am the gate. Whoever enters by me will be saved, and will come in and go out and find pasture. The thief comes only to steal and kill and destroy. I came that they may have life, and have it abundantly.

*Prayer*

Lord God, you call us each by name in the first moment of life;
You call us day by day into your love and life;
You call each of us to be your presence in our world.
Help me to say yes to this call daily in life;
Help others to find you through who I am and what I do. Amen.

*Reflection*

Jesus talks a lot about giving life and about the fullness of life. It's not just for hereafter. Eternal life is our faith in him, and in his word. His call is to be life-givers – to facilitate the full life of compassion, justice, reconciliation and peace. We are called to be ministers of life, serving the God who loves all life. To live in faith is to share the eternal life of God.

## Fourth Sunday of Easter Year B

*John 10:11-18*

'I am the good shepherd. The good shepherd lays down his life for the sheep. The hired hand, who is not the shepherd and does not own the sheep, sees the wolf coming and leaves the sheep and runs away – and the wolf snatches them and scatters them. The hired hand runs away because a hired hand does not care for the sheep. I am the good shepherd. I know my own and my own know me, just as the Father knows me and I know the Father. And I lay down my life for the sheep. I have other sheep that do not belong to this fold. I must bring them also, and they will listen to my voice. So there will be one flock, one shepherd. For this reason the Father loves me, because I lay down my life in order to take it up again. No one takes it from me, but I lay it down of my own accord. I have power to lay it down, and I have power to take it up again. I have received this command from my Father.'

## Prayer

Lord God, you call us each by name in the first
moment of life;
You call us day by day into your love and life;
You call each of us to be your presence in our
world.
Help me to say yes to this call daily in life;
Help others to find you through who I am and
what I do. Amen.

## Reflection

Jesus talks a lot about giving life and about the
fullness of life. It's not just for hereafter. Eternal
life is our faith in him, and in his word. His call
is to be life-givers – to facilitate the full life of
compassion, justice, reconciliation and peace.
We are called to be ministers of life, serving the
God who loves all life. To live in faith is to
share the eternal life of God.

## Fourth Sunday of Easter Year C

*John 10:27-30*

'My sheep hear my voice. I know them, and they follow me. I give them eternal life, and they will never perish. No one will snatch them out of my hand. What my Father has given me is greater than all else, and no one can snatch it out of the Father's hand. The Father and I are one.'

## Prayer

Lord God, you call us each by name in the first
moment of life;

You call us day by day into your love and life;

You call each of us to be your presence in our
world.

Help me to say yes to this call daily in life;

Help others to find you through who I am and
what I do. Amen.

## Reflection

Jesus talks a lot about giving life and about the
fullness of life. It's not just for hereafter. Eternal
life is our faith in him, and in his word. His call
is to be life-givers – to facilitate the full life of
compassion, justice, reconciliation and peace.
We are called to be ministers of life, serving the
God who loves all life. To live in faith is to
share the eternal life of God.

## Week 4: Monday

*John 10:1-10*

Jesus said to the people: 'Very truly, I tell you, anyone who does not enter the sheepfold by the gate but climbs in by another way is a thief and a bandit. The one who enters by the gate is the shepherd of the sheep. The gatekeeper opens the gate for him, and the sheep hear his voice. He calls his own sheep by name and leads them out. When he has brought out all his own, he goes ahead of them, and the sheep follow him because they know his voice. They will not follow a stranger, but they will run from him because they do not know the voice of strangers.' Jesus used this figure of speech with them, but they did not understand what he was saying to them. So again Jesus said to them, 'Very truly, I tell you, I am the gate for the sheep. All who came before me are thieves and bandits; but the sheep did not listen to them. I am the gate. Whoever enters by me will be saved, and will come in and go out and find pasture. The thief comes only to steal and kill and destroy. I came that they may have life, and have it abundantly.

*Prayer*

Lord God, you call us each by name in the first
moment of life;
You call us day by day into your love and life;
You call each of us to be your presence in our
world.
Help me to say yes to this call daily in life;
Help others to find you through who I am and
what I do. Amen.

*Reflection*

We are hearers of many voices – the interior
voices which call us to the full life of Jesus, the
other voices which keep us stuck in 'living and
partly living', or the voice which leads us to
evil. Jesus knows that goodness does not
always reign, and that the evil in people
spreads into violence and indignity and greed.
Prayer can purify so that we hear the good, dis-
cern the voices and commit ourselves to the
good.

## Week 4: Tuesday

*John 10:22-30*

Jesus said to the people: 'I am the good shepherd; I know my own and my own know me, just as the Father knows me and I know the Father; and I lay down my life for my sheep. There are other sheep I have that are not of this fold, and I must lead these too. They too will listen to my voice, and there will be only one flock, one shepherd.'

*Prayer*

Lord God, you call us each by name in the first
moment of life;
You call us day by day into your love and life;
You call each of us to be your presence in our
world.
Help me to say yes to this call daily in life;
Help others to find you through who I am and
what I do. Amen.

*Reflection*

Jesus wants to lead us to safety, to the fullness
of life and wants us to listen to his voice. He
waits for our time, to enter the space of our life
which is his. Time with Jesus is never wasted,
whether in listening to his word, mulling over
it, or just being with him in peaceful silence.
Prayer is the comforting relationship of a sheep
with a shepherd, relaxing into the mystery of
being loved by God.

## Week 4: Wednesday

*John 12:44-50*

Then Jesus cried aloud: 'Whoever believes in me believes not in me but in him who sent me. And whoever sees me sees him who sent me. I have come as light into the world, so that everyone who believes in me should not remain in the darkness.'

## Prayer

Lord God, you call us each by name in the first
moment of life;

You call us day by day into your love and life;

You call each of us to be your presence in our
world.

Help me to say yes to this call daily in life;

Help others to find you through who I am and
what I do. Amen.

## Reflection

Jesus points us to something more than human,
from within the human. Humanity is lit up by
him, enlightened by its creator, so that we
know that within our human personality is the
spark of divinity. Jesus became like us so that
we might become like him. The light of God
shines through all creation, bringing life, compassion, justice. It is a caring light, caring for
humanity, caring for creation.

## Week 4: Thursday

*John 13:16-20*
After Jesus had washed their feet, had put on
his robe, and had returned to the table, he said
to them, 'Do you know what I have done to
you? You call me Teacher and Lord – and you
are right, for that is what I am. So if I, your Lord
and Teacher, have washed your feet, you also
ought to wash one another's feet. For I have set
you an example, that you also should do as I
have done to you.'

### Prayer

Lord God, you call us each by name in the first
moment of life;
You call us day by day into your love and life;
You call each of us to be your presence in our
world.
Help me to say yes to this call daily in life;
Help others to find you through who I am and
what I do. Amen.

### Reflection

This is the light of God shining through the
serving love of Jesus. When we allow ourselves
be served by God – this is the meaning of the
gesture of washing their feet – we are bathed in
humble and bright light. The light which Jesus
shone through his life is now ours to share.
Without his disciples now, the light of God will
be dim if not extinguished. Light of Christ,
enlighten me, enlighten the world.

## Week 4: Friday

*John 14:1-6*
Jesus said to the disciples, 'Do not let your
hearts be troubled. Believe in God, believe also
in me. In my Father's house there are many
dwelling-places. If it were not so, would I have
told you that I go to prepare a place for you?
And if I go and prepare a place for you, I will
come again and will take you to myself, so that
where I am, there you may be also. And you
know the way to the place where I am going.'
Thomas said to him, 'Lord, we do not know
where you are going. How can we know the
way?' Jesus said to him, 'I am the way, and the
truth, and the life. No one comes to the Father
except through me.'

## *Prayer*

Lord God, you call us each by name in the first
moment of life;

You call us day by day into your love and life;

You call each of us to be your presence in our
world.

Help me to say yes to this call daily in life;

Help others to find you through who I am and
what I do. Amen.

## *Reflection*

One of the big identity statements of Jesus is in
these words of the gospel. Without any ifs and
buts, he declares himself as the way, truth and
life. God is accessible through him because he
is God. These words are a gift: that with him
we have the deepest personal security in life,
knowing that all can be found in him.

## Week 4: Saturday

*John 14:7-14*

Jesus said, 'If you know me, you will know my Father also. From now on you do know him and have seen him.' Philip said to him, 'Lord, show us the Father, and we will be satisfied.' Jesus said to him, 'Have I been with you all this time, Philip, and you still do not know me? Whoever has seen me has seen the Father. How can you say, "Show us the Father"? Do you not believe that I am in the Father and the Father is in me? The words that I say to you I do not speak on my own; but the Father who dwells in me does his works. Believe me that I am in the Father and the Father is in me; but if you do not, then believe me because of the works themselves. Very truly, I tell you, the one who believes in me will also do the works that I do and, in fact, will do greater works than these, because I am going to the Father. I will do whatever you ask in my name, so that the Father may be glorified in the Son. If in my name you ask me for anything, I will do it.'

*Prayer*

Lord God, you call us each by name in the first
moment of life;
You call us day by day into your love and life;
You call each of us to be your presence in our
world.
Help me to say yes to this call daily in life;
Help others to find you through who I am and
what I do. Amen.

*Reflection*

When we pray, something goes on deep inside
us. Without being able to articulate it, we get to
know God. Everyone who prays knows God.
Some of the deepest faith is in people who just
know in the heart that God is near, that God is
caring and that God is love, and that everything in life can make sense. We can try too
hard in prayer to reach God; the movement of
prayer is that God reaches us, and when we
sense that, we know we are immensely gifted.

## Fifth Sunday in Easter Year A

*John 14:1-12*

Jesus said, 'Do not let your hearts be troubled. Believe in God, believe also in me. In my Father's house there are many dwelling-places. If it were not so, would I have told you that I go to prepare a place for you? And if I go and prepare a place for you, I will come again and will take you to myself, so that where I am, there you may be also. And you know the way to the place where I am going.' Thomas said to him, 'Lord, we do not know where you are going. How can we know the way?' Jesus said to him, 'I am the way, and the truth, and the life. No one comes to the Father except through me.

*Prayer*

Unite me with yourself, Lord Jesus;
make me one with the Spirit of love
who exists always and everywhere.
Give me always the joy of being one with you.
Bless also all whom I remember and will meet
this day. Amen.

*Reflection*

The gospel presents Jesus as the guide in life, as
the 'way, truth and life'. The Christian centre is
the person of Christ. Our work for Jesus and
our love for people, no matter what our calling
in life, flow from this. This centre always holds,
it cannot be unhinged. It is a deeply personal
relationship: we are led by Jesus 'one by one',
known by name, not as just one of a group. We
follow him as one we know, not a stranger.
Studying his life and times, getting to know the
places and events of his life, becoming familiar
with the gospels and getting to know him in
the heart in prayer is the way of keeping our
centre of conviction and motivation strong. As
this happens freedom grows and we begin to
find him everywhere.

## Fifth Sunday in Easter Year B

*John 15:1-8b*
I am the true vine, and my Father is the vine-grower. He removes every branch in me that bears no fruit. Every branch that bears fruit he prunes to make it bear more fruit. You have already been cleansed by the word that I have spoken to you. Abide in me as I abide in you. Just as the branch cannot bear fruit by itself unless it abides in the vine, neither can you unless you abide in me. I am the vine, you are the branches. Those who abide in me and I in them bear much fruit, because apart from me you can do nothing. Whoever does not abide in me is thrown away like a branch and withers; such branches are gathered, thrown into the fire, and burned. If you abide in me, and my words abide in you, ask for whatever you wish, and it will be done for you. My Father is glorified by this, that you bear much fruit and become my disciples.

*Prayer*
Unite me with yourself, Lord Jesus;
make me one with the Spirit of love
who exists always and everywhere.
Give me always the joy of being one with you.
Bless also all whom I remember and will meet
this day. Amen.

*Reflection*
The closeness of the relationship with ourselves and Jesus is like branch and tree. One
gives life to the other and draws life from the
other. A real relationship with Jesus is life-giving – it is loving, healing and challenging. It
brings life to the soul and energy to the body.
The relationship itself bears fruit and brings to
each of us a loving and energetic quality of life.

## Fifth Sunday of Easter Year C

*John 13:31-35*

When he had gone out, Jesus said, 'Now the Son of Man has been glorified, and God has been glorified in him. If God has been glorified in him, God will also glorify him in himself and will glorify him at once. Little children, I am with you only a little longer. You will look for me; and as I said to the Jews so now I say to you, 'Where I am going, you cannot come.' I give you a new commandment, that you love one another. Just as I have loved you, you also should love one another. By this everyone will know that you are my disciples, if you have love for one another.'

### Prayer

Unite me with yourself, Lord Jesus;
make me one with the Spirit of love
who exists always and everywhere.
Give me always the joy of being one with you.
Bless also all whom I remember and will meet
this day. Amen.

### Reflection

They were looking for Jesus as many looked
before and after Good Friday – some to kill
him, others to follow him. We look in many
places for God, and find God in creation,
prayer and very ordinary signs of his presence.
We find him also in discipleship – in following
the words and lifestyle of the gospel. Thus we
find him in love, which is how we know we are
disciples.

## Week 5: Monday

*John 14:21-26*

Jesus said,'They who have my commandments and keep them are those who love me; and those who love me will be loved by my Father, and I will love them and reveal myself to them.' Judas (not Iscariot) said to him, 'Lord, how is it that you will reveal yourself to us, and not to the world?' Jesus answered him, 'Those who love me will keep my word, and my Father will love them, and we will come to them and make our home with them. Whoever does not love me does not keep my words; and the word that you hear is not mine, but is from the Father who sent me. I have said these things to you while I am still with you. But the Advocate, the Holy Spirit, whom the Father will send in my name, will teach you every-thing, and remind you of all that I have said to you.'

*Prayer*

Unite me with yourself, Lord Jesus;
make me one with the Spirit of love
who exists always and everywhere.
Give me always the joy of being one with you.
Bless also all whom I remember and will meet
this day. Amen.

*Reflection*

The image of home is strong in the gospel –
Jesus visited  the house of Zacchaeus, and the
home of Peter, and makes home in each of us.
He knocks at the door and waits to be invited
into our space and our lives. He is not a crowd-
ing visitor but one who accepts what he sees
and enjoys our welcome. Prayer is our time of
welcoming Jesus into our day and our lives.

## Week 5: Tuesday

*John 14:27-31*
Jesus said to his disciples: 'Peace I leave with you; my peace I give to you. I do not give to you as the world gives. Do not let your hearts be troubled, and do not let them be afraid. Rise, let us be on our way.'

*Prayer*

Unite me with yourself, Lord Jesus;
make me one with the Spirit of love
who exists always and everywhere.
Give me always the joy of being one with you.
Bless also all whom I remember and will meet
this day. Amen.

*Reflection*

Peace can exist in the heart at times of great turmoil and trouble, pain and illness. The peace of Christ invades us gently and fills the spaces of our personality, which are open to peace and often need peace. It is the peace of healing and forgiveness, and the peace which comes from doing what we know to be our calling. Sometimes within the toughest times of life we can sense this peace of Jesus.

## Week 5: Wednesday

*John 15:1-8*
I am the true vine, and my Father is the vine-grower. He removes every branch in me that bears no fruit. Every branch that bears fruit he prunes to make it bear more fruit. You have already been cleansed by the word that I have spoken to you. Abide in me as I abide in you. Just as the branch cannot bear fruit by itself unless it abides in the vine, neither can you unless you abide in me. I am the vine, you are the branches. Those who abide in me and I in them bear much fruit, because apart from me you can do nothing. Whoever does not abide in me is thrown away like a branch and withers; such branches are gathered, thrown into the fire, and burned. If you abide in me, and my words abide in you, ask for whatever you wish, and it will be done for you. My Father is glorified by this, that you bear much fruit and become my disciples.

### Prayer

Unite me with yourself, Lord Jesus;
make me one with the Spirit of love
who exists always and everywhere.
Give me always the joy of being one with you.
Bless also all whom I remember and will meet
this day. Amen.

### Reflection

When we try to do good in our lives and live
according to the word of God and the gospel of
Jesus, God helps us. He removes what is no
good in me with love and grace, and makes my
gifts and qualities of love and service grow
even more if I give him the chance. God is cre-
ating each of us every day, growing us in love
and service. We need just to be there, to allow
ourselves be reached by him in prayer, and be
touched in heart and soul each day by the word
of Jesus.

## Week 5: Thursday

*John 15:9-11*
Jesus said to his disciples, 'As the Father has loved me, so I have loved you; abide in my love. If you keep my commandments, you will abide in my love, just as I have kept my Father's commandments and abide in his love. I have said these things to you so that my joy may be in you, and that your joy may be complete.'

## Prayer

Unite me with yourself, Lord Jesus;
make me one with the Spirit of love
who exists always and everywhere.
Give me always the joy of being one with you.
Bless also all whom I remember and will meet
this day. Amen.

## Reflection

The place of these words of Jesus is at the last
supper, so the writers are giving a pride of
place to them – among his last words. Last
words of anyone are generally well remembered. The full place of love in the Christian life
is highlighted. All else flows from the love of
God and ourselves, uniting us together. Love of
this kind leads to joy. We see Jesus as one who
gifts us with joy and with love.

## Friday: Week 5

*John 15:12-17*

This is my commandment, that you love one another as I have loved you. No one has greater love than this, to lay down one's life for one's friends. You are my friends if you do what I command you. I do not call you servants any longer, because the servant does not know what the master is doing; but I have called you friends, because I have made known to you everything that I have heard from my Father. You did not choose me but I chose you. And I appointed you to go and bear fruit, fruit that will last, so that the Father will give you whatever you ask him in my name. I am giving you these commands so that you may love one another.

*Prayer*

Unite me with yourself, Lord Jesus;
make me one with the Spirit of love
who exists always and everywhere.
Give me always the joy of being one with you.
Bless also all whom I remember and will meet
this day. Amen.

*Reflection*

The love of Jesus is self-sacrificing love, seen on the cross. Where best to see love than at Calvary? The love of Calvary is love for all, and wants and desires that we know and receive this love. In prayer we might imagine ourselves at Calvary and allow the love of Jesus Christ be given to each of us.

## Week 5: Saturday

*John 15:18-21*

If the world hates you, be aware that it hated me before it hated you. If you belonged to the world, the world would love you as its own. Because you do not belong to the world, but I have chosen you out of the world, therefore the world hates you. Remember the word that I said to you, 'Servants are not greater than their master. If they persecuted me, they will persecute you; if they kept my word, they will keep yours also. But they will do all these things to you on account of my name, because they do not know him who sent me. If I had not come and spoken to them, they would not have sin; but now they have no excuse for their sin. Whoever hates me hates my Father also. If I had not done among them the works that no one else did, they would not have sin. But now they have seen and hated both me and my Father. It was to fulfil the word that is written in their law, 'They hated me without a cause'.

*Prayer*

Unite me with yourself, Lord Jesus;
make me one with the Spirit of love
who exists always and everywhere.
Give me always the joy of being one with you.
Bless also all whom I remember and will meet
this day. Amen.

*Reflection*

Not everyone accepts Jesus, which was his experience from the start. Opposition to him took him to death, and love took him from death to resurrection. Persecution and similar opposition is the experience of many of his followers. Goodness sometimes offends people; evil can be for a while stronger than love, but the message of Jesus is that love conquers all.

## Sixth Sunday of Easter Year A

*John 14:1-12*

'Do not let your hearts be troubled. Believe in God, believe also in me. In my Father's house there are many dwelling-places. If it were not so, would I have told you that I go to prepare a place for you? And if I go and prepare a place for you, I will come again and will take you to myself, so that where I am, there you may be also. And you know the way to the place where I am going.' Thomas said to him, 'Lord, we do not know where you are going. How can we know the way?' Jesus said to him, 'I am the way, and the truth, and the life. No one comes to the Father except through me. If you know me, you will know my Father also. From now on you do know him and have seen him.'

Philip said to him, 'Lord, show us the Father, and we will be satisfied.' Jesus said to him, 'Have I been with you all this time, Philip, and you still do not know me? Whoever has seen me has seen the Father. How can you say, "Show us the Father"? Do you not believe that I am in the Father and the Father is in me? The words that I say to you I do not speak on my own; but the Father who dwells in me does his works. Believe me that I am in the Father and the Father is in me; but if you do not, then believe me because of the works themselves.

Very truly, I tell you, the one who believes in me will also do the works that I do and, in fact, will do greater works than these, because I am going to the Father.

## Prayer

May your love arise each day in me, O Lord;
May your risen life bring joy, peace and healing in all I am;
May your risen life through me bring joy, peace and healing to all I meet.
Amen.

## Reflection

We need guides on the way, teachers of truth and givers of life. We find this in Jesus – he guides us, enightens us and love us. He guides us to himself, teaches us of himself and gives us himself. This can be a source of satisfying and full meaning in life; it can be also seen as the love of the Father, the guidance of the Son and the truth of the Spirit.

## Sixth Sunday of Easter Year B

*John 15:9-17*

Jesus said to his disciples, 'As the Father has loved me, so I have loved you; abide in my love. If you keep my commandments, you will abide in my love, just as I have kept my Father's commandments and abide in his love. I have said these things to you so that my joy may be in you, and that your joy may be complete. This is my commandment, that you love one another as I have loved you. No one has greater love than this, to lay down one's life for one's friends. You are my friends if you do what I command you. I do not call you servants any longer, because the servant does not know what the master is doing; but I have called you friends, because I have made known to you everything that I have heard from my Father. You did not choose me but I chose you. And I appointed you to go and bear fruit, fruit that will last, so that the Father will give you whatever you ask him in my name. I am giving you these commands so that you may love one another.

*Prayer*

May your love arise each day in me, O Lord;
May your risen life bring joy, peace and healing
in all I am;
May your risen life through me bring joy, peace
and healing to all I meet.
Amen.

*Reflection*

The place of these words of Jesus is at the Last Supper, so the writers are giving a pride of place to them – among his last words. Last words of anyone are generally well remembered. The full place of love in the Christian life is highlighted. All else flows from the love of God and ourselves uniting us together. Love of this kind leads to joy. We see Jesus as one who gifts us with joy and with love.

## Sixth Sunday of Easter Year C

*John 14:23-29*

Jesus said to his disciples, 'Those who love me will keep my word, and my Father will love them, and we will come to them and make our home with them. Whoever does not love me does not keep my words; and the word that you hear is not mine, but is from the Father who sent me.'

'I have said these things to you while I am still with you. But the Advocate, the Holy Spirit, whom the Father will send in my name, will teach you everything, and remind you of all that I have said to you. Peace I leave with you; my peace I give to you. I do not give to you as the world gives. Do not let your hearts be troubled, and do not let them be afraid. You heard me say to you, 'I am going away, and I am coming to you.' If you loved me, you would rejoice that I am going to the Father, because the Father is greater than I. And now I have told you this before it occurs, so that when it does occur, you may believe.'

*Prayer*

May your love arise each day in me, O Lord;
May your risen life bring joy, peace and healing
in all I am;
May your risen life through me bring joy, peace
and healing to all I meet. Amen.

*Reflection*

The way of Jesus is the way of fullest human
love, completion and fulfilment. His commands are not just for our duty, but are the
path to joy and love in life. The love he means
is the love that is welcoming, accepting and
forgiving of others, as best we can. It is the love
that joins his followers together. Without this
love, the following of Jesus is empty and dry.
His way of life is not just taught but shown to
us by the way he lives.

## Week 6: Monday

*John 15:26-16:4*
Jesus said, 'When the Advocate comes, whom I will send to you from the Father, the Spirit of truth who comes from the Father, he will testify on my behalf. You also are to testify because you have been with me from the beginning. I have said these things to you to keep you from stumbling. They will put you out of the synagogues. Indeed, an hour is coming when those who kill you will think that by doing so they are offering worship to God. And they will do this because they have not known the Father or me. But I have said these things to you so that when their hour comes you may remember that I told you about them. I did not say these things to you from the beginning, because I was with you.'

## *Prayer*

May your love arise each day in me, O Lord;
May your risen life bring joy, peace and healing
in all I am;
May your risen life through me bring joy, peace
and healing to all I meet. Amen.

## *Reflection*

Jesus taught his disciples with his word, and prepared them for life when he would no longer be with them. He knew that there would be opposition to them and danger to their lives because of their following of him. Banishment from their places of worship will bring them to remember what he told them. Prayer is listening over and over again to the word of God so that it becomes part of us like our daily food and daily bread.

## Week 6: Tuesday

*John 16:5-11*

Jesus said, 'Now I am going to him who sent me; yet none of you asks me, "Where are you going?" But because I have said these things to you, sorrow has filled your hearts. Nevertheless, I tell you the truth: it is to your advantage that I go away, for if I do not go away, the Advocate will not come to you; but if I go, I will send him to you. And when he comes, he will prove the world wrong about sin and righteousness and judgement: about sin, because they do not believe in me; about righteousness, because I am going to the Father and you will see me no longer; about judgement, because the ruler of this world has been condemned.'

## *Prayer*

May your love arise each day in me, O Lord;
May your risen life bring joy, peace and healing
in all I am;
May your risen life through me bring joy, peace
and healing to all I meet. Amen.

## *Reflection*

There is a new world ahead of the disciples –
the world of the Spirit who will speak within
them for the convictions and the love of God in
Jesus. The Spirit of truth is not tied to time or
space and inspires in all time the desire to live
by truth and follow the Lord Jesus.

## Week 6: Wednesday

*John 16:12-15*

Jesus said, 'I still have many things to say to you, but you cannot bear them now. When the Spirit of truth comes, he will guide you into all the truth; for he will not speak on his own, but will speak whatever he hears, and he will declare to you the things that are to come. He will glorify me, because he will take what is mine and declare it to you. All that the Father has is mine. For this reason I said that he will take what is mine and declare it to you.'

### *Prayer*

May your love arise each day in me, O Lord;
May your risen life bring joy, peace and healing
in all I am;
May your risen life through me bring joy, peace
and healing to all I meet. Amen.

### *Reflection*

Jesus does not abandon the one who followed
him. Earthly death does not confine his word to
the era of the first century. Jesus, through his
Spirit, is still our guide and our way, truth and
life. The Spirit unites heaven and earth, God
and humanity, within each person and within
each community of Jesus Christ.

## Week 6: Thursday

*John 16:16-20*

Jesus said to his disciples, 'A little while, and you will no longer see me, and again a little while, and you will see me.' Then some of his disciples said to one another, 'What does he mean by saying to us, "A little while, and you will no longer see me, and again a little while, and you will see me"; and "Because I am going to the Father"?' They said, 'What does he mean by this "a little while"? We do not know what he is talking about.' Jesus knew that they wanted to ask him, so he said to them, 'Are you discussing among yourselves what I meant when I said, "A little while, and you will no longer see me, and again a little while, and you will see me"? Very truly, I tell you, you will weep and mourn, but the world will rejoice; you will have pain, but your pain will turn into joy.'

### Prayer

May your love arise each day in me, O Lord;
May your risen life bring joy, peace and healing
in all I am;
May your risen life through me bring joy, peace
and healing to all I meet. Amen.

### Reflection

Pain turning into joy is part of the human con-
dition. A grain of wheat falls and dies in the
ground and then becomes a rich harvest. Loss
and pain can bring closeness – to God and to
each other. It may not. Prayer can be a time of
noticing the good in everything and of praying
that pain will turn into joy and that evil may
give way to good.

## Week 6: Friday

*John 16:20-23*

Jesus said to his disciples, 'Very truly, I tell you, you will weep and mourn, but the world will rejoice; you will have pain, but your pain will turn into joy. When a woman is in labour, she has pain, because her hour has come. But when her child is born, she no longer remembers the anguish because of the joy of having brought a human being into the world. So you have pain now; but I will see you again, and your hearts will rejoice, and no one will take your joy from you. On that day you will ask nothing of me. Very truly, I tell you, if you ask anything of the Father in my name, he will give it to you.'

### Prayer

May your love arise each day in me, O Lord;
May your risen life bring joy, peace and healing
in all I am;
May your risen life through me bring joy, peace
and healing to all I meet. Amen.

### Reflection

Pain and the varied difficulties of life need not
be the final word for the follower of Jesus. Pain
often turns to joy, and in every small 'death' in
life is the hope of rising into a deeper life with
Jesus. Problems can be a path towards growth,
especially in the context of love; they may also
be a cul-de-sac, blocking any future develop-
ment and joy. With Jesus we walk always with
the Alleluia on our lips and in our hearts.

## Week 6: Saturday

*John 16:23-28*

Jesus said to his disciples, 'Very truly, I tell you, if you ask anything of the Father in my name, he will give it to you. Until now you have not asked for anything in my name. Ask and you will receive, so that your joy may be complete. I have said these things to you in figures of speech. The hour is coming when I will no longer speak to you in figures, but will tell you plainly of the Father. On that day you will ask in my name. I do not say to you that I will ask the Father on your behalf; for the Father himself loves you, because you have loved me and have believed that I came from God. I came from the Father and have come into the world; again, I am leaving the world and am going to the Father.'

*Prayer*

May your love arise each day in me, O Lord;
May your risen life bring joy, peace and healing
in all I am;
May your risen life through me bring joy, peace
and healing to all I meet. Amen.

*Reflection*

We ask often in prayer and sometimes prayer is
answered very directly. Even when this appears
not to happen, no prayer, like no act in love, is
wasted. The true gift of prayer is always the
Father's love, given to us no matter what we
ask for. We are always gifted with the Spirit of
Jesus, alive in our lives and in our love. We ask
always in his name, knowing that in his name
God will always hear us, inspire us, direct us
and love us.

## Seventh Sunday of Easter Year A
## Ascension of Our Lord

*Matthew 28:16-20*

Now the eleven disciples went to Galilee, to the mountain to which Jesus had directed them. When they saw him, they worshiped him; but some doubted. And Jesus came and said to them, 'All authority in heaven and on earth has been given to me. Go therefore and make disciples of all nations, baptising them in the name of the Father and of the Son and of the Holy Spirit, and teaching them to obey everything that I have commanded you. And remember, I am with you always, to the end of the age.'

### Prayer

You are raised to joy and new life,
Lord hear my prayer;
You are raised to the glory of your Father,
Lord hear my prayer;
Lord, you are present among us in your holy
Spirit,
Lord hear my prayer.
Risen Lord, thank you for life, for love, for
mercy. Amen.

### Reflection

A man went out on a starry night and shook his
fist at the heavens yelling, 'Oh, God, what a
lousy, rotten world you've made. I could have
done much better.' Then a voice boomed from
the clouds saying, 'That's why I put you there.
Get busy.' The Ascension is the time when
Jesus puts us in charge of his mission and his
work, promising to be always with us. Prayer
can be a time of asking and discovering where
each can work in this world.

## Seventh Sunday of Easter Year B
## Ascension of Our Lord

*Mark 16:15-20*

And Jesus said to the disciples, 'Go into all the world and proclaim the good news to the whole creation. The one who believes and is baptised will be saved; but the one who does not believe will be condemned. And these signs will accompany those who believe: by using my name they will cast out demons; they will speak in new tongues; they will pick up snakes in their hands, and if they drink any deadly thing, it will not hurt them; they will lay their hands on the sick, and they will recover.' So then the Lord Jesus, after he had spoken to them, was taken up into heaven and sat down at the right hand of God. And they went out and proclaimed the good news everywhere, while the Lord worked with them and confirmed the message by the signs that accompanied it.

*Prayer*

You are raised to joy and new life,
Lord hear my prayer;
You are raised to the glory of your Father,
Lord hear my prayer;
Lord, you are present among us in your holy
Spirit,
Lord hear my prayer.
Risen Lord, thank you for life, for love, for
mercy. Amen.

*Reflection*

A man went out on a starry night and shook his
fist at the heavens yelling, 'Oh, God, what a
lousy, rotten world you've made. I could have
done much better.' Then a voice boomed from
the clouds saying, 'That's why I put you there.
Get busy.' The Ascension is the time when
Jesus puts us in charge of his mission and his
work, promising to be always with us. Prayer
can be a time of asking and discovering where
each can work in this world.

## Seventh Sunday of Easter Year C
## Ascension of Our Lord

*Luke 24:46-53*

Then he opened their minds to understand the scriptures, and he said to them, 'Thus it is written, that the Messiah is to suffer and to rise from the dead on the third day, and that repentance and forgiveness of sins is to be proclaimed in his name to all nations, beginning from Jerusalem. You are witnesses of these things. And see, I am sending upon you what my Father promised; so stay here in the city until you have been clothed with power from on high.' Then he led them out as far as Bethany, and, lifting up his hands, he blessed them. While he was blessing them, he withdrew from them and was carried up into heaven. And they worshipped him, and returned to Jerusalem with great joy; and they were continually in the temple blessing God.

*Prayer*

You are raised to joy and new life,
Lord hear my prayer;
You are raised to the glory of your Father,
Lord hear my prayer;
Lord, you are present among us in your holy Spirit,
Lord hear my prayer.
Risen Lord, thank you for life, for love, for mercy. Amen.

*Reflection*

A man went out on a starry night and shook his fist at the heavens yelling, 'Oh, God, what a lousy, rotten world you've made. I could have done much better.' Then a voice boomed from the clouds saying, 'That's why I put you there. Get busy.' The Ascension is the time when Jesus puts us in charge of his mission and his work, promising to be always with us. Prayer can be a time of asking and discovering where each can work in this world.

## Week 7: Monday

*John 16:29-33*

His disciples said, 'Yes, now you are speaking plainly, not in any figure of speech! Now we know that you know all things, and do not need to have anyone question you; by this we believe that you came from God.' Jesus answered them, 'Do you now believe? The hour is coming, indeed it has come, when you will be scattered, each one to his home, and you will leave me alone. Yet I am not alone because the Father is with me. I have said this to you, so that in me you may have peace. In the world you face persecution. But take courage; I have conquered the world!'

### Prayer

You are raised to joy and new life,
Lord hear my prayer;
You are raised to the glory of your Father,
Lord hear my prayer;
Lord, you are present among us in your holy
Spirit,
Lord hear my prayer.
Risen Lord, thank you for life, for love, for
mercy. Amen.

### Reflection

These words of Jesus are the foundation and
basis for Christian hope. Our hope in life is
based on the victory of Jesus over death, and
on his ongoing presence in our lives. His is a
saving and energising presence, and gives the
courage and conviction we develop in prayer.
He has conquered anything that can make for
discouragement and despair.

## Week 7: Tuesday

*John 17:1-11*

After Jesus had spoken these words, he looked up to heaven and said, 'Father, the hour has come; glorify your Son so that the Son may glorify you, since you have given him authority over all people, to give eternal life to all whom you have given him. And this is eternal life, that they may know you, the only true God, and Jesus Christ whom you have sent.'

### Prayer

You are raised to joy and new life,
Lord hear my prayer;
You are raised to the glory of your Father,
Lord hear my prayer;
Lord, you are present among us in your holy
Spirit,
Lord hear my prayer.
Risen Lord, thank you for life, for love, for
mercy. Amen.

### Reflection

Eternal life is not just for the future; it is a gift
partly given now in our faith. To be in touch
with Jesus is to be in touch with a rich, full,
eternal life. Something is given which will last
forever, the mysterious life of God. We touch
into that life in prayer like living water, new
sight, and are enlightened by the light of the
world.

## Week 7: Wednesday

*John 17:11-19*
Jesus said to the disciples, 'And now I am no longer in the world, but they are in the world, and I am coming to you. Holy Father, protect them in your name that you have given me, so that they may be one, as we are one. While I was with them, I protected them in your name that you have given me. I guarded them, and not one of them was lost except the one destined to be lost, so that the scripture might be fulfilled. But now I am coming to you, and I speak these things in the world so that they may have my joy made complete in themselves. I have given them your word, and the world has hated them because they do not belong to the world, just as I do not belong to the world. I am not asking you to take them out of the world, but I ask you to protect them from the evil one. They do not belong to the world, just as I do not belong to the world. Sanctify them in the truth; your word is truth. As you have sent me into the world, so I have sent them into the world. And for their sakes I sanctify myself, so that they also may be sanctified in truth.'

*Prayer*

You are raised to joy and new life,
Lord hear my prayer;
You are raised to the glory of your Father,
Lord hear my prayer;
Lord, you are present among us in your holy Spirit,
Lord hear my prayer.
Risen Lord, thank you for life, for love, for mercy. Amen.

*Reflection*

Jesus is like a good friend here. He wants to keep us with him, just as none of us want to lose a friend. Friendship with Jesus is being with him, and being sent in his name. Our mission as his followers is in the midst and in the depths of the world. He wants his love and message inserted in the centre of the world, the city, the neighbourhood. In following him in mission and love, we are ourselves sanctified. Prayer helps and completes this daily sanctification, growing in closeness to him.

## Week 7: Thursday

*John 17:20-26*

Jesus looked up to heaven and said, 'I ask not only on behalf of these, but also on behalf of those who will believe in me through their word, that they may all be one. As you, Father, are in me and I am in you, may they also be in us, so that the world may believe that you have sent me. The glory that you have given me I have given them, so that they may be one, as we are one, I in them and you in me, that they may become completely one, so that the world may know that you have sent me and have loved them even as you have loved me. Father, I desire that those also, whom you have given me, may be with me where I am, to see my glory, which you have given me because you loved me before the foundation of the world. Righteous Father, the world does not know you, but I know you; and these know that you have sent me. I made your name known to them, and I will make it known, so that the love with which you have loved me may be in them, and I in them.'

*Prayer*

You are raised to joy and new life,
Lord hear my prayer;
You are raised to the glory of your Father,
Lord hear my prayer;
Lord, you are present among us in your holy
Spirit,
Lord hear my prayer.
Risen Lord, thank you for life, for love, for
mercy. Amen.

*Reflection*

This is the prayer of Jesus for his followers
through the ages. Jesus prays for each of us.
Can we imagine him at prayer, and he is naming his apostles and his friends and all he
wants to pray for? Prayer is our naming of
God; it is also Jesus' naming of us to his Father.
Let him name you. Even take a thought for
what he might pray for you. In opening ourselves to prayer, we are opening ourselves to
Jesus praying for us. Sit and silently allow his
prayer for you take over your heart.

## Week 7: Friday

*John 21:15-19*

When they had finished breakfast, Jesus said to Simon Peter, 'Simon son of John, do you love me more than these?' He said to him, 'Yes, Lord; you know that I love you.' Jesus said to him, 'Feed my lambs.' A second time he said to him, 'Simon son of John, do you love me?' He said to him, 'Yes, Lord; you know that I love you.' Jesus said to him, 'Tend my sheep.' He said to him the third time, 'Simon son of John, do you love me?' Peter felt hurt because he said to him the third time, 'Do you love me?' And he said to him, 'Lord, you know everything; you know that I love you.' Jesus said to him, 'Feed my sheep. Very truly, I tell you, when you were younger, you used to fasten your own belt and to go wherever you wished. But when you grow old, you will stretch out your hands, and someone else will fasten a belt around you and take you where you do not wish to go.' (He said this to indicate the kind of death by which he would glorify God.) After this he said to him, 'Follow me.'

*Prayer*
You are raised to joy and new life,
Lord hear my prayer;
You are raised to the glory of your Father,
Lord hear my prayer;
Lord, you are present among us in your holy
Spirit,
Lord hear my prayer.
Risen Lord, thank you for life, for love, for
mercy. Amen.

*Reflection*
Many people repeat often in prayer, 'Lord you
know I love you.' It's a humble prayer because
often we feel we don't live up to our call from
God or to the goodness of love we receive in
life. We may feel the shame Peter felt on looking at his history of denying his friend, Jesus.
God looks into the heart and sees what we
would like to be, as well as seeing what we
have done in life. Prayer is giving time to be
aware that God is looking into our hearts and
loving us for who we are.

## Week 7: Saturday

*John 21:20-25*

Peter turned and saw the disciple whom Jesus loved following them; he was the one who had reclined next to Jesus at the supper and had said, 'Lord, who is it that is going to betray you?' When Peter saw him, he said to Jesus, 'Lord, what about him?' Jesus said to him, 'If it is my will that he remain until I come, what is that to you? Follow me!' So the rumour spread in the community that this disciple would not die. Yet Jesus did not say to him that he would not die, but, 'If it is my will that he remain until I come, what is that to you?' This is the disciple who is testifying to these things and has written them, and we know that his testimony is true. But there are also many other things that Jesus did; if every one of them were written down, I suppose that the world itself could not contain the books that would be written.

*Prayer*

You are raised to joy and new life,
Lord hear my prayer;
You are raised to the glory of your Father,
Lord hear my prayer;
Lord, you are present among us in your holy Spirit,
Lord hear my prayer.
Risen Lord, thank you for life, for love, for mercy. Amen.

*Reflection*

Each bible has a blank page at the end. This is for each of us to write our own gospel! We can note the incidents, relationships, bad times and good in our lives where Jesus was close, active, saving us, calling us and challenging us into discipleship. Can you note where and when your life with Jesus begin? Like John, we don't know where it will end. Where now is Jesus writing his gospel in your life so that others will know is love, his call and his identity? Some good pointers for prayer!

## Pentecost Sunday

*John 20:19-23*

When it was evening on that day, the first day of the week, and the doors of the house where the disciples had met were locked for fear of the Jews, Jesus came and stood among them and said, 'Peace be with you.' After he said this, he showed them his hands and his side. Then the disciples rejoiced when they saw the Lord. Jesus said to them again, 'Peace be with you. As the Father has sent me, so I send you.' When he had said this, he breathed on them and said to them, 'Receive the Holy Spirit. If you forgive the sins of any, they are forgiven them; if you retain the sins of any, they are retained.'

## *Prayer*

Holy Spirit breathe your life and love around me;
Let the breath of your life fill my life.
Holy Spirit, this is a prayer for your gifts –
Gentleness, patience, integrity, compassion
And, above all, love. Amen.

## *Reflection*

Unity is not easy. It is not just similarity. Unity doesn't mean we all pretend all is well. It's living with, accepting, even enjoying differences. Some differences are too much for friendship or family but we can still value the other and not fight. The past does not disappear. As unity demands tolerance, at times it will demand forgiveness and a wish for healing and freedom. At other times if we are to get along side by side it means reconciliation, and a new relationship. The Spirit in each of us can help unity. Pray for someone you are at odds with – believe that he or she has the Spirit of God like you. It helps! This is some of the Spirit of Pentecost.